THANK *You*

IN APPRECIATION OF YOU, AND ALL THAT YOU DO.

COMPENDIUM™
INCORPORATED

live inspired.

ACKNOWLDEGEMENTS

These quotations were gathered lovingly but unscientifically over several years and/or were contributed by many friends or acquaintances. Some arrived and survived in our files on scraps of paper and may therefore be imperfectly worded or attributed. To the authors, contributors and original sources, our thanks, and where appropriate, our apologies. —The Editors

WITH SPECIAL THANKS TO

Jason Aldrich, Gloria Austin, Gerry Baird, Jay Baird, Neil Beaton, Josie Bissett, Laura Boro, Chris Dalke, Jim and Alyssa Darragh & Family, Jennifer and Matt Ellison & Family, Rob Estes, Michael and Leianne Flynn & Family, Sarah Forster, Heidi Jones, Carol Anne Kennedy, June Martin, Jessica Phoenix and Tom DesLongchamp, Steve and Janet Potter & Family, Diane Roger, Kirsten and Garrett Sessions, Kristel Wills, Clarie Yam and Erik Lee, Kobi and Heidi Yamada & Family, Justi and Tote Yamada & Family, Bob and Val Yamada, Kaz and Kristin Yamada & Family, Tai and Joy Yamada, Anne Zadra, August and Arline Zadra, and Gus and Rosie Zadra.

CREDITS
Compiled by Dan Zadra
Designed by Jenica Wilkie
Dedicated to Jennifer Hurwitz

IN APPRECIATION OF YOU,
AND ALL THAT YOU DO.

How lucky we are! Past or present, if we stop to think about all the people who have made a difference in our lives, we can't help but feel a warm sense of gratitude.

Did someone walk you home from school when you were little? Who sat up with you all night when you were sick? Who taught you how to catch a fish, or kick the ball, or carry a tune? Who talked you out of quitting the team, or talked you into getting a degree?

Who knew you way back when? Who believed in you before you believed in yourself? Who gave you your first break, or your first order, or bet on your company, or told you how good you could really be?

Who cheered you on when you were winning, or cheered you up when you were down? Who thought of you when everyone else was thinking of themselves?

Thinking back on my own life, I realize that some of the people who were so good to me are gone now. Did I thank them? I don't think so, but I meant to.

Yesterday is gone forever, but today is a great day for all of us to stop and express our sincere thanks to those who change our lives for the better. Treasured friends, family, customers, or colleagues—whoever's at the top of your thank you list— write a personal note in this book and let them know how much you appreciate who they are and all that they do.

Dan Zadra

THANK YOU FOR

WE MUST FIND TIME TO STOP
AND THANK THE PEOPLE WHO
MAKE A DIFFERENCE IN OUR LIVES.

DAN ZADRA

THERE ARE PEOPLE WHO TAKE THE
HEART OUT OF YOU, AND THERE ARE
PEOPLE WHO PUT IT BACK.

ELIZABETH DAVID

BE GRATEFUL, TRULY GRATEFUL,
FOR THOSE GOOD FRIENDS OR
THOUGHTFUL PEOPLE.

SHAWNA CORLEY

THERE ARE HIGH SPOTS IN ALL OF
OUR LIVES, AND MOST OF THEM COME
ABOUT THROUGH ENCOURAGEMENT
FROM SOMEONE ELSE.

GEORGE ADAMS

ONE DOESN'T KNOW, TILL ONE
IS A BIT AT ODDS WITH THE WORLD,
HOW MUCH ONE'S FRIENDS WHO
BELIEVE IN ONE RATHER
GENEROUSLY, MEAN TO ONE.

9

D.H. LAWRENCE

IF THE PEOPLE AROUND YOU DON'T
BELIEVE IN YOU, IF THEY DON'T
ENCOURAGE YOU, THEN YOU NEED
TO FIND SOME PEOPLE WHO DO.

JOHN MAXWELL

SOMEBODY SAW SOMETHING
IN YOU ONCE—AND THAT IS WHY
YOU'RE WHERE YOU ARE TODAY.
THANK THEM!

DON WARD

LONG BEFORE I WAS A SUCCESS,
MY PARENTS MADE ME FEEL
LIKE I COULD BE ONE.

TONI MORRISON

I MADE YOU A KITE SO YOU
WOULD HAVE TO LOOK UP.

UNKNOWN

I THINK MY PARENTS RECOGNIZED
SOMETHING IN ME THAT THEY
ENCOURAGED INSTEAD OF DEFLATED,
AND I'LL ALWAYS BE GRATEFUL
TO THEM FOR THAT.

GRAHAM NASH

11

I WAS LUCKY TO BE BROUGHT
UP LOVED. NOT THAT EVERYTHING I
DID WAS LIKED, BUT I KNEW THAT I
WAS LOVED—AND KNOWING THIS GAVE
ME THE ABILITY AND FREEDOM TO
BE WHO I WANTED TO BE.

BERNIE SIEGEL

WE ALL HAVE THE EXTRAORDINARY
CODED WITHIN US, WAITING
TO BE RELEASED.

JEAN HOUSTON

12

MOST PEOPLE SEE WHAT IS,
AND NEVER SEE WHAT CAN BE.

ALBERT EINSTEIN

IT REQUIRES THE EYE OF
FAITH TO SEE THE UNDEVELOPED
BUTTERFLY IN THE CATERPILLAR.

MARGARET LARSON

FAITH HELPS YOU SUCCEED
WHEN EVERYTHING ELSE FAILS.

DAWN EWING

MY MOTHER TAUGHT ME VERY
EARLY ON TO BELIEVE I COULD
ACHIEVE ANY ACCOMPLISHMENT
I WANTED TO. THE FIRST WAS
TO WALK WITHOUT BRACES.

WILMA RUDOLPH

13

THANK YOU FOR BELIEVING
IN ME BEFORE I BELIEVED
IN MYSELF.

KOBI YAMADA

A GOOD TEACHER IS ONE
WHO HELPS YOU BECOME WHO
YOU FEEL YOURSELF TO BE.

JULIUS LESTER

14

YOU MUST BELIEVE IN YOURSELF,
MY CHILD, OR NO ONE ELSE WILL
BELIEVE IN YOU. BE SELF-CONFIDENT,
SELF-RELIANT, AND EVEN IF YOU DON'T
MAKE IT, YOU WILL KNOW YOU HAVE
DONE YOUR BEST. NOW GO TO IT.

MARY HARDY MacARTHUR

IF I HAVE THE BELIEF THAT I CAN
DO IT, I SHALL SURELY ACQUIRE
THE CAPACITY TO DO IT.

MAHATMA GANDHI

15

VIRTUALLY EVERY GREAT
ACCOMPLISHMENT OR MOVEMENT
WAS STARTED BY SOMEONE WHO
BELIEVED PASSIONATELY IN SOMETHING—
AND SOMEONE WHO BELIEVED
PASSIONATELY IN THAT PERSON.

MARGARET WARREN

SURROUND YOURSELF WITH
PEOPLE WHO BELIEVE YOU CAN.

DAN ZADRA

THOSE WHO BELIEVE IN
OUR ABILITY DO MORE THAN
STIMULATE US. THEY CREATE FOR US
AN ATMOSPHERE IN WHICH IT
BECOMES EASIER TO SUCCEED.

JOHN SPALDING

16

BY CHOOSING TO BELIEVE AND
EXPECT THE BEST ABOUT PEOPLE,
YOU ARE ABLE TO BRING OUT
THE BEST IN THEM.

BOB MOAWAD

THE GREATEST GOOD WE CAN DO
FOR OTHERS IS NOT TO SHARE OUR
RICHES BUT TO REVEAL THEIRS.

UNKNOWN

FAR AWAY THERE IN THE SUNSHINE
ARE MY HIGHEST ASPIRATIONS. I MAY
NOT REACH THEM, BUT I CAN LOOK UP
AND SEE THEIR BEAUTY, BELIEVE IN THEM,
AND TRY TO FOLLOW WHERE THEY LEAD.

LOUISA MAY ALCOTT

17

SOMEWHERE SOMEONE IS
LOOKING FOR EXACTLY WHAT
YOU HAVE TO OFFER.

LOUISE L. HAY

SOMETIMES OUR LIGHT GOES
OUT BUT IS BLOWN INTO FLAME BY
ANOTHER HUMAN BEING. EACH OF US
OWES DEEPEST THANKS TO THOSE
WHO HAVE REKINDLED THIS LIGHT.

ALBERT SCHWEITZER

18

THANKS FOR SHOWING ME THAT
EVEN ON THE DARKEST, RAINIEST
DAYS THE SUN IS STILL THERE,
JUST BEHIND THE CLOUDS,
WAITING TO SHINE AGAIN.

LISA HARLOW

I'D LIKE TO DO THE BIG THINGS
AND THE SPLENDID THINGS FOR YOU,
TO BRUSH THE GRAY FROM OUT YOUR
SKIES AND LEAVE THEM ONLY BLUE.

EDGAR GUEST

TWO PERSONS MUST BELIEVE
IN EACH OTHER, AND FEEL THAT
IT CAN AND MUST BE DONE—
THAT WAY THEY ARE ENORMOUSLY
STRONG. THEY MUST KEEP EACH
OTHER'S COURAGE UP.

VINCENT VAN GOGH

19

BELIEVE THAT THERE'S LIGHT
AT THE END OF THE TUNNEL.
BELIEVE THAT YOU MIGHT BE THAT
LIGHT FOR SOMEONE ELSE.

KOBI YAMADA

THANK YOU FOR

caring

CARING IS EVERYTHING;
NOTHING MATTERS BUT CARING.

FRIEDRICH VON HÜGEL

WHAT MATTERS TODAY IS NOT
THE DIFFERENCE BETWEEN THOSE
WHO BELIEVE AND THOSE WHO DO
NOT BELIEVE, BUT THE DIFFERENCE
BETWEEN THOSE WHO CARE
AND THOSE WHO DON'T.

ABBÉ PIRE

22

I WILL ACT AS IF I DO
MAKE A DIFFERENCE.

WILLIAM JAMES

WHEN YOU CARE,
PEOPLE NOTICE.

SUSANE BERGER

DO THE KINDS OF THINGS THAT
COME FROM THE HEART. WHEN YOU
DO, YOU WON'T BE DISSATISFIED,
YOU WON'T BE ENVIOUS, YOU WON'T
BE LONGING FOR SOMEBODY ELSE'S
THINGS. ON THE CONTRARY, YOU'LL
BE OVERWHELMED WITH WHAT
COMES BACK.

MORRIE SCHWARTZ

23

SMALL TOKENS OF SINCERE
CONSIDERATION OR LOVE CARRY
MESSAGES FAR BEYOND THEIR SIZE.

KARL-HANS VON FREMDE

THE MANNER OF GIVING IS
WORTH MORE THAN THE GIFT.

PIERRE CORNEILLE

24

TOO OFTEN WE UNDERESTIMATE
THE POWER OF A TOUCH, A SMILE,
A KIND WORD, OR THE SMALLEST ACT
OF CARING, ALL OF WHICH HAVE THE
POTENTIAL TO TURN A LIFE AROUND.

LEO BUSCAGLIA

WHEN WE RECALL THE PAST,
WE USUALLY FIND THAT IT IS THE
SIMPLEST THINGS—NOT THE GREAT
OCCASIONS—THAT IN RETROSPECT
GIVE OFF THE GREATEST
GLOW OF HAPPINESS.

BOB HOPE

25

WE CANNOT EXPLAIN WHY
THESE LITTLE SIGNS MEAN SO
MUCH TO US. BUT THE FACT IS
THAT A WORD OF THANKS FOR
SOME SMALL THING CAN
TRANSFORM OUR DAY.

JEANNE REIDY

CARING IS A POWERFUL
BUSINESS ADVANTAGE.

SCOTT JOHNSON

TAKE PRIDE IN WHAT YOU DO.
THE KIND OF PRIDE I'M TALKING
ABOUT IS NOT THE ARROGANT
PUFFED-UP KIND; IT'S JUST THE
WHOLE IDEA OF CARING—
FIERCELY CARING.

RED AUERBACH

CARE MORE THAN OTHERS
THINK WISE. RISK MORE THAN
OTHERS THINK SAFE. DREAM MORE
THAN OTHERS THINK PRACTICAL.
EXPECT MORE THAN OTHERS
THINK POSSIBLE.

UNKNOWN

26

LOVE PEOPLE. USE THINGS.
NOT VICE-VERSA.

KELLY ANN ROTHAUS

IT'S HUMAN NATURE TO
THINK ABOUT OURSELVES.
IT'S HUMAN RELATIONS TO
THINK ABOUT OTHERS.

BOB MOAWAD

27

I USE THE BUSINESS TO
MAKE GREAT PEOPLE. I DON'T
USE PEOPLE TO MAKE A
GREAT BUSINESS.

RALPH STAYER

A MAN IS ONLY AS
GOOD AS WHAT HE LOVES.

SAUL BELLOW

WHEN YOU LOVE YOUR WORK,
IT SHOWS.

AUDREY WOODHALL

28

KNOW WHAT YOU ARE DOING.
LOVE WHAT YOU ARE DOING.
BELIEVE IN WHAT YOU ARE DOING.

STEVE MUSSEAU

WHEN I GIVE,
I GIVE MYSELF.

WALT WHITMAN

PEOPLE WANT TO MAKE A
DIFFERENCE AND BE RESPECTED.
IS THAT A SURPRISE?

PAUL AMES

IF PEOPLE BELIEVE IN THE
COMPANY THEY WORK FOR,
THEY POUR THEIR HEART INTO
MAKING IT BETTER.

HOWARD SCHULTZ

THE GREATEST TRAGEDY
IS INDIFFERENCE.

THE RED CROSS

SEVEN NATIONAL CRIMES:
I DON'T THINK. I DON'T KNOW.
I DON'T CARE. I AM TOO BUSY.
I LEAVE WELL ENOUGH ALONE.
I HAVE NO TIME TO READ AND
FIND OUT. I AM NOT INTERESTED.

WILLIAM J.H. BOETCKER

30

IF WE HAVE NO PEACE,
IT IS BECAUSE WE HAVE
FORGOTTEN THAT WE
BELONG TO EACH OTHER.

MOTHER TERESA

YOU REALLY CAN
CHANGE THE WORLD IF
YOU CARE ENOUGH.

MARIAN W. EDELMAN

I BELIEVE THAT ONE OF THE
MOST IMPORTANT THINGS TO LEARN
IN LIFE IS THAT YOU CAN MAKE A
DIFFERENCE IN YOUR COMMUNITY
NO MATTER WHO YOU ARE OR WHERE
YOU LIVE. I HAVE SEEN SO MANY GOOD
DEEDS—PEOPLE HELPED, LIVES IMPROVED—
BECAUSE SOMEONE CARED.

ROSALYNN CARTER

SOME PEOPLE MAKE
THE WORLD MORE SPECIAL
JUST BY BEING IN IT.

KELLY ANN ROTHAUS

A MOTHER IS A PERSON WHO,
SEEING THERE ARE ONLY FOUR
PIECES OF PIE FOR FIVE PEOPLE,
PROMPTLY ANNOUNCES SHE
NEVER DID CARE FOR PIE.

TENNEVA JORDAN

CHILDREN WILL NOT REMEMBER
YOU FOR THE MATERIAL THINGS
YOU PROVIDED BUT FOR THE FEELING
THAT YOU CHERISHED THEM.

GAIL GRENIER SWEET

IT IS LOVELY, WHEN I FORGET
ALL BIRTHDAYS, INCLUDING MY
OWN, TO FIND THAT SOMEBODY
REMEMBERS ME.

ELLEN GLASGOW

I AM SO GLAD YOU ARE HERE...
IT HELPS ME TO REALIZE HOW
BEAUTIFUL MY WORLD IS.

RAINER MARIA RILKE

33

THE HUMAN HEART, AT
WHATEVER AGE, OPENS
TO THE HEART THAT
OPENS IN RETURN.

MARIA EDGEWORTH

WHAT WE DO TODAY,
RIGHT NOW, WILL HAVE AN
ACCUMULATED EFFECT ON ALL
OF OUR TOMORROWS.

ALEXANDRA STODDARD

SIMPLY GIVE OTHERS A BIT
OF YOURSELF; A THOUGHTFUL
ACT, A HELPFUL IDEA, A WORD OF
APPRECIATION, A LIFT OVER A
ROUGH SPOT, A SENSE OF
UNDERSTANDING, A
TIMELY SUGGESTION.

CHARLES H. BURR

WHEN I COUNT MY BLESSINGS,
I COUNT YOU TWICE.

IRISH PROVERB

TAKE GOOD CARE OF YOURSELF,
JUST AS YOU HAVE TAKEN SUCH
GOOD CARE OF OTHERS.

35

DAN ZADRA

TREASURE THIS DAY,
AND TREASURE YOURSELF.
TRULY, NEITHER WILL
EVER HAPPEN AGAIN.

RAY BRADBURY

THANK YOU FOR

pporting

YOU CAN'T BE HUMAN ALONE.

MARGARET KUHN

NO ONE CAN GO IT ALONE.
SOMEWHERE ALONG THE LINE IS
THE PERSON WHO GIVES YOU FAITH
THAT YOU CAN MAKE IT.

GRACE GIL OLIVAREZ

38

MY HEART GIVES THANKS FOR
EMPTY MOMENTS GIVEN TO DREAMS,
AND FOR THOUGHTFUL PEOPLE WHO
HELP THOSE DREAMS COME TRUE.

WILLIAM S. BRAITHWAITE

SURROUND YOURSELF WITH
PEOPLE WHO RESPECT YOU
AND TREAT YOU WELL.

CLAUDIA BLACK

THERE IS A PLACE FOR EVERYONE
IN THE BIG PICTURE. TO TURN YOUR
BACK ON ANY ONE PERSON, FOR
WHATEVER REASON, IS TO RUN THE
RISK OF LOSING THE CENTRAL
PIECE OF YOUR JIGSAW PUZZLE.

JOHNNA HOWELL

39

THOSE WHOM WE SUPPORT
HOLD US UP IN LIFE.

MARIE VON EBNER-ESCHENBACH

I GET BY WITH A LITTLE
HELP FROM MY FRIENDS.

JOHN LENNON

CHERISH YOUR HUMAN
CONNECTIONS—YOUR RELATIONSHIPS
WITH FRIENDS AND FAMILY.

BARBARA BUSH

40

THE GLUE OF LIFE AND WORK
IS LOVING SUPPORT.

ESTELLE FREDERICKSON

MENTOR EACH
OTHER UNSELFISHLY.

"HEROIC ENVIRONMENTS"

FRIENDS ARE KIND TO EACH
OTHER'S HOPES. THEY CHERISH
EACH OTHER'S DREAMS.

HENRY DAVID THOREAU

41

IF SOMEONE LISTENS, OR
STRETCHES OUT A HAND, OR
WHISPERS A KIND WORD OF
ENCOURAGEMENT, OR ATTEMPTS
TO UNDERSTAND, EXTRAORDINARY
THINGS BEGIN TO HAPPEN.

LORETTA GIRZARTIS

ALONE WE CAN DO SO LITTLE,
TOGETHER WE CAN DO SO MUCH.

HELEN KELLER

THE NICE THING ABOUT
TEAMWORK IS THAT YOU ALWAYS
HAVE OTHERS ON YOUR SIDE.

MARGARET CARTY

DRAW STRENGTH FROM
EACH OTHER.

JAMES A. RENIER

THE IDEA IS NOT TO SEE
THROUGH ONE ANOTHER, BUT TO
SEE ONE ANOTHER THROUGH.

C.D. JACKSON

LOYALTY MEANS NOT THAT
I AGREE WITH EVERYTHING YOU SAY,
OR THAT I BELIEVE YOU ARE ALWAYS
RIGHT. LOYALTY MEANS THAT I SHARE
A COMMON IDEAL WITH YOU AND THAT,
REGARDLESS OF MINOR DIFFERENCES,
WE STRIVE FOR IT, SHOULDER TO
SHOULDER, CONFIDENT IN ONE
ANOTHER'S GOOD FAITH, TRUST,
CONSTANCY, AND AFFECTION.

DR. KARL A. MENNINGER

43

FRIENDS ARE THOSE RARE
PEOPLE WHO ASK HOW WE
ARE, AND THEN WAIT TO
HEAR THE ANSWER.

ED CUNNINGHAM

MY FRIEND PICKED ME UP
WHEN I WAS DOWN, MADE ME LAUGH
THOUGH MY EYES WERE FULL OF
TEARS, HELD ME CLOSE WHEN THERE
WAS NOTHING ELSE TO DO.

LISA WILLOW

MY HEART IS FILLED WITH
LOVE AND CARE, THAT GREW FROM
SEEDS YOU PLANTED THERE.

DEBBIE TOMASSI

IT TAKES EACH OF US
TO MAKE A DIFFERENCE
FOR ALL OF US.

JACKIE MUTCHESON

HAVE I EVER TOLD YOU YOU'RE
MY HERO? YOU'RE EVERYTHING
I WOULD LIKE TO BE. I CAN CLIMB
HIGHER THAN AN EAGLE. YOU ARE
THE WIND BENEATH MY WINGS.

LARRY HENLEY & JEFF SILBAR

45

ALL ARE NEEDED BY EACH ONE:
NOTHING IS FAIR OR GOOD ALONE.

RALPH WALDO EMERSON

IF YOU'RE SCARED,
JUST HOLLER AND YOU'LL
FIND IT AIN'T SO
LONESOME OUT THERE.

JOE SUGDEN

46

SO COME STAND BY MY SIDE
WHERE I AM GOING, TAKE MY
HAND IF I STUMBLE AND FALL,
IT'S THE STRENGTH THAT YOU
SHARE WHEN YOU'RE GROWING,
THAT GIVES ME WHAT I
NEED MOST OF ALL.

HOYT AXTON

I'LL LEAN ON YOU AND YOU
LEAN ON ME AND WE'LL BE OKAY.

DAVE MATTHEWS BAND

IT'S THE FRIENDS YOU
CAN CALL UP AT 4 A.M.
THAT MATTER.

MARLENE DIETRICH

WHEN FRIENDS ASK,
THERE IS NO TOMORROW...
ONLY NOW.

ALEXANDER DREY

47

TAKE CARE OF THOSE WHO
TAKE CARE OF YOU.

TONY NICCOLI

THERE IS NO "THEM AND US."
IN A WORLD THIS SIZE THERE
CAN ONLY BE "WE"—ALL OF US
WORKING TOGETHER.

DON WARD

IT MAY BE IN FACT UTTERLY
IMPOSSIBLE TO BE SUCCESSFUL
WITHOUT HELPING ANOTHER PERSON
TO BECOME SUCCESSFUL. I DON'T
KNOW. BUT I DON'T THINK ONE CAN
BECOME LIBERATED WITHOUT
LIBERATING SOMEBODY ELSE.

MAYA ANGELOU

THE WHOLE IS THE SUM OF
THE PARTS. BE A GOOD PART.

NATE McCONNELL

WE ALL NEED SOMEBODY
TO LEAN ON.

BILL WITHERS

EVERYONE STANDS ALONE AT
THE HEART OF THE WORLD
PIERCED BY A RAY OF SUNLIGHT,
AND SUDDENLY IT IS EVENING.

SALVATORE QUASIMODO

49

ARE YOU LOOKING FOR ME?
I AM IN THE NEXT SEAT.
MY SHOULDER IS AGAINST YOURS.

KABIR

THANK YOU FOR

LIFE IS NOT EASY FOR ANY OF US.

MARIE CURIE

52

ENCOURAGE MEANS "TO GIVE SOMEONE COURAGE." THIS IS A POWER WE ALL HAVE, AND IT'S NOT DIFFICULT, AND ANYONE CAN DO IT. WHEN I WAS AT MY LOWEST EBB AND HAD DECIDED TO GIVE UP WRITING, MY SIX-YEAR-OLD ANGELA CAME TO ME AND SAID, "YOU MUSTN'T QUIT, DADDY, I WON'T ALLOW IT." AND THAT'S HOW MY FIRST BEST-SELLER GOT ITS LIFE.

MIGUEL SANTABASILE

BUT EVERY ROAD IS ROUGH TO ME
THAT HAS NO FRIEND TO CHEER IT.

ELIZABETH SHANE

MOST OF US, SWIMMING AGAINST
THE TIDES OF TROUBLES THE WORLD
KNOWS NOTHING ABOUT, NEED ONLY A
BIT OF PRAISE OR ENCOURAGEMENT—
AND WE'LL MAKE THE GOAL.

J.P. FLEISHMAN

53

KIND WORDS CAN BE SHORT
AND EASY TO SPEAK, BUT THEIR
ECHOES ARE TRULY ENDLESS.

MOTHER TERESA

ANYONE CAN BLAME;
IT TAKES A SPECIALIST TO PRAISE.

KONSTANTIN STANISLAVSKI

54

THOSE WHO ARE LIFTING THE
WORLD UPWARD AND ONWARD
ARE THOSE WHO ENCOURAGE
MORE THAN CRITICIZE.

ELIZABETH HARRISON

ENCOURAGEMENT IS THE
OXYGEN OF THE SOUL.

GEORGE M. ADAMS

IN LIFE'S DARKEST
MOMENTS, A TINY SPARK
CAN LIGHT THE WAY.

"SHADES OF GRACE"

THANK GOD THERE WERE
A COUPLE PEOPLE IN MY LIFE
WHO SAID, "GO ON, GO ON—
YOU CAN DO IT."

BARBRA STREISAND

YOUR SPARK CAN
BECOME A FLAME AND
CHANGE EVERYTHING.

E.D. NIXON

ENCOURAGE ONE ANOTHER.
MANY TIMES A WORD OF PRAISE
OR THANKS OR APPRECIATION
OR CHEER HAS KEPT PEOPLE
ON THEIR FEET.

CHARLES SWINDOLL

56 NEVER GIVE UP ON ANYBODY.

HUBERT H. HUMPHREY

FEW THINGS IN THE WORLD
ARE MORE POWERFUL THAN
A POSITIVE PUSH. A SMILE. A
WORD OF OPTIMISM AND HOPE.
A "YOU CAN DO IT" WHEN
THINGS ARE TOUGH.

RICHARD M. DEVOS

MY BEST FRIEND IS THE
ONE WHO BRINGS OUT
THE BEST IN ME.

HENRY FORD

A TRUE FRIEND IS ONE WHO
SUPPORTS YOU WHEN YOU ARE
STRUGGLING, PRODS YOU TO
PERSONAL GROWTH, AND
CELEBRATES YOUR SUCCESSES
AS IF THEY WERE HIS OWN.

RICHARD EXLEY

57

SOMETIMES THE BEST HELPING
HAND YOU CAN GIVE IS A
GOOD, FIRM PUSH.

UNKNOWN

KEEP AWAY FROM PEOPLE WHO
TRY TO BELITTLE YOUR AMBITIONS.
SMALL PEOPLE ALWAYS DO THAT,
BUT THE REALLY GREAT MAKE
YOU FEEL THAT YOU, TOO,
CAN BECOME GREAT.

MARK TWAIN

58

REALIZE HOW GOOD
YOU REALLY ARE.

OG MANDINO

ENCOURAGE EACH OTHER TO
BECOME THE BEST YOU CAN BE.
CELEBRATE WHAT YOU WANT
TO SEE MORE OF.

TOM PETERS

MANAGERS LIGHT A FIRE
UNDER PEOPLE; LEADERS
LIGHT A FIRE IN PEOPLE.

KATHY AUSTIN

THOSE WITH WHOM WE
WORK LOOK TO US FOR HEAT
AS WELL AS LIGHT.

WOODROW WILSON

BE A GOOD-FINDER.
TRY TO CATCH PEOPLE
RED-HANDED IN THE ACT OF
DOING SOMETHING RIGHT.

BOB MOAWAD

PRAISE IS JUST LETTING
OFF A LITTLE ESTEEM.

MICHAEL NOLAN

NOTHING ELSE CAN QUITE
SUBSTITUTE FOR A FEW WELL-
CHOSEN, WELL-TIMED, SINCERE
WORDS OF PRAISE. THEY'RE
ABSOLUTELY FREE—AND
WORTH A FORTUNE.

SAM WALTON

60

THE FIVE MOST IMPORTANT WORDS:
"YOU DID A GREAT JOB."

UNKNOWN

PEOPLE ARE IN GREATER NEED
OF YOUR PRAISE WHEN THEY TRY
AND FAIL, THAN WHEN THEY
TRY AND SUCCEED.

UNKNOWN

WE SHALL NEVER KNOW
ALL THE GOOD THAT A
SIMPLE SMILE CAN DO.

MOTHER TERESA

MILLIONS OF PEOPLE GO
TO BED HUNGRY FOR A KIND WORD,
A PAT ON THE BACK, OR A SMILE.
THAT'S WHERE YOU CAN
MAKE A DIFFERENCE.

A.C. CARLSON

YOU HAVE THE POWER
TO MAKE SOMEONE'S DAY.

DAN ZADRA

YOU CANNOT ALWAYS HAVE
HAPPINESS, BUT YOU CAN
ALWAYS GIVE HAPPINESS.

UNKNOWN

62

I WILL SPEAK ILL OF NO ONE,
AND SPEAK ALL THE GOOD I
KNOW OF EVERYONE.

BENJAMIN FRANKLIN

BRING JOY TO ONE PERSON
IN THE MORNING AND EASE THE
PAIN OF ANOTHER IN THE EVENING.

BUDDHIST SAYING

IF YOU WANT OTHERS TO
BE HAPPY, PRACTICE COMPASSION.
IF YOU WANT TO BE HAPPY,
PRACTICE COMPASSION.

THE DALAI LAMA

63

MAKE ONE PERSON HAPPY
EACH DAY AND IN FORTY YEARS
YOU WILL HAVE MADE 14,600
HUMAN BEINGS HAPPY FOR A
LITTLE TIME AT LEAST.

CHARLEY WILLEY

THANK YOU FOR

THE ONLY PEOPLE TO GET
EVEN WITH ARE THOSE WHO
HAVE HELPED US.

UNKNOWN

WE ARE ALL HERE ON EARTH
TO HELP OTHERS; WHAT ON
EARTH THE OTHERS ARE HERE
FOR I DON'T KNOW.

W. H. AUDEN

WHEN A FRIEND IS IN
TROUBLE, DON'T ANNOY HIM
BY ASKING IF THERE IS ANYTHING
YOU CAN DO. THINK UP SOMETHING
APPROPRIATE AND DO IT.

EDGAR WATSON HOWE

MANY ARE CALLED
BUT FEW GET UP.

OLIVER HERFORD

IF LOVE IS TRULY A VERB, IF
HELP IS A VERB, IF FORGIVENESS
IS A VERB, IF KINDNESS IS A
VERB, THEN YOU CAN DO
SOMETHING ABOUT IT.

BETTY EADIE

67

ANY GOOD THAT I CAN DO,
LET ME DO IT NOW.

STEPHEN GRELLET

GREAT OPPORTUNITIES TO
HELP OTHERS SELDOM COME,
BUT SMALL ONES SURROUND
US EVERY DAY.

SALLY KOCH

SOMETIMES WHEN I CONSIDER
WHAT TREMENDOUS CONSEQUENCES
COME FROM LITTLE THINGS—
A CHANCE WORD, A TAP ON THE
SHOULDER—I AM TEMPTED TO THINK...
THERE ARE NO LITTLE THINGS.

BRUCE BARTON

THERE ARE NO LITTLE THINGS.
"LITTLE THINGS" ARE THE
HINGES OF THE UNIVERSE.

FANNY FERN

SMALL DEEDS DONE
ARE BETTER THAN GREAT
DEEDS PLANNED.

PETER MARSHALL

ALL WE CAN ASK IN OUR
LIVES IS THAT PERHAPS WE CAN
MAKE A LITTLE DIFFERENCE
IN SOMEONE ELSE'S.

LILLIAN DAVIS

69

WE'RE ALL TRYING TO MAKE A
BIG DIFFERENCE, NOT REALIZING
THE SMALL DIFFERENCE WE MAKE
FOR EACH OTHER EVERY DAY.

DAPHNE ROSE KINGMA

LIFE'S MOST PERSISTENT AND
URGENT QUESTION IS: WHAT ARE
YOU DOING FOR OTHERS?

MARTIN LUTHER KING, JR.

DOING NOTHING FOR OTHERS
IS THE UNDOING OF ONE'S SELF.
WE MUST BE PURPOSELY KIND AND
GENEROUS OR WE MISS THE BEST
PART OF EXISTENCE.

HORACE MANN

THE WELFARE OF EACH IS
BOUND UP IN THE WELFARE OF ALL.

HELEN KELLER

SOME PEOPLE STRENGTHEN
OUR SOCIETY JUST BY BEING
THE KIND OF PEOPLE THEY ARE.

JOHN W. GARDNER

I THINK WE NEED TO LOOK
FOR COMMUNITY BY FEELING
COMPASSIONATELY WHAT OTHERS ARE
GOING THROUGH AND RESPONDING
WITH OUR TIME AND HEARTS.

THOMAS MOORE

IN EVERY COMMUNITY, THERE IS
WORK TO BE DONE. IN EVERY NATION,
THERE ARE WOUNDS TO HEAL.
IN EVERY HEART, THERE IS THE
POWER TO DO IT.

MARIANNE WILLIAMSON

THERE IS NO SUCH THING
AS A SELF-MADE MAN. YOU WILL
REACH YOUR GOALS ONLY
WITH THE HELP OF OTHERS.

GEORGE SHINN

NO MATTER WHAT
ACCOMPLISHMENTS YOU MAKE
IN LIFE, SOMEBODY HELPS YOU.

WILMA RUDOLPH

MANY HANDS, HEARTS, AND
MINDS GENERALLY CONTRIBUTE
TO ANYONE'S NOTABLE
ACHIEVEMENTS.

WALT DISNEY

VERY FEW BURDENS ARE
HEAVY IF EVERYONE LIFTS.

SY WISE

THE WORLD IS MOVED ALONG,
NOT ONLY BY THE MIGHTY SHOVES
OF ITS HEROES, BUT ALSO BY THE
AGGREGATE OF THE TINY PUSHES
OF EACH HONEST WORKER.

HELEN KELLER

73

TEAMWORK THRIVES WHEN
NO ONE POINTS A FINGER,
AND EVERYONE LENDS A HAND.

DAN ZADRA

IT IS ONE OF THE MOST BEAUTIFUL
COMPENSATIONS OF LIFE, THAT NO
MAN CAN SINCERELY TRY TO HELP
ANOTHER WITHOUT HELPING HIMSELF.

RALPH WALDO EMERSON

74

AS LONG AS YOU ARE DOING
GOOD THINGS FOR OTHER PEOPLE,
OTHER PEOPLE WILL DO GOOD
THINGS FOR YOU.

BRIAN TRACY

TO FALL DOWN, YOU MANAGE
ALONE, BUT IT TAKES FRIENDLY
HANDS TO GET UP.

YIDDISH PROVERB

GOODWILL IS RECIPROCAL.
THE GOOD THOUGHTS YOU SEND
OUT TO OTHERS WILL RETURN
TO YOU MULTIPLIED.

GRENVILLE KLEISER

ONE LEAVES BEHIND A
LITTLE OF ONESELF AT ANY
HOUR, ANY PLACE.

EDMOND HARAUCOURT

75

WE DO NOT EXPERIENCE,
AND THUS HAVE NO MEASURE
OF THE DISASTERS WE
HAVE PREVENTED.

JOHN KENNETH GALBRAITH

LET NO ONE EVER
COME TO YOU WITHOUT
LEAVING BETTER.

MOTHER TERESA

NEVER, IF POSSIBLE, LIE DOWN
AT NIGHT WITHOUT BEING ABLE TO
SAY: I HAVE MADE ONE HUMAN BEING,
AT LEAST, A LITTLE WISER, A LITTLE
HAPPIER, OR A LITTLE BETTER THIS DAY.

CHARLES KINGSLEY

WHEN YOU ARE KIND TO SOMEONE
IN TROUBLE, YOU HOPE THEY'LL
REMEMBER AND BE KIND TO SOMEONE
ELSE...IT'LL BECOME LIKE A WILDFIRE.

WHOOPI GOLDBERG

A LIFE IS NOT IMPORTANT,
EXCEPT IN THE IMPACT IT
HAS ON OTHER LIVES.

JACKIE ROBINSON

FEW WILL HAVE THE GREATNESS TO
BEND HISTORY ITSELF, BUT EACH OF
US CAN WORK TO CHANGE A SMALL
PORTION OF EVENTS, AND IN THE TOTAL
OF ALL THOSE ACTS WILL BE WRITTEN
THE HISTORY OF THIS GENERATION.

ROBERT F. KENNEDY

A GREAT LIFE IS THE SUM TOTAL
OF THE WORTHWHILE THINGS
YOU'VE BEEN DOING ONE BY ONE.

RICHARD BACH

THE MEASURE OF A LIFE,
AFTER ALL, IS NOT ITS DURATION
BUT ITS DONATION.

PETER MARSHALL

EVERYWHERE IN LIFE THE TRUE
QUESTION IS, NOT WHAT WE HAVE
GAINED, BUT WHAT WE DO.

THOMAS CARLYLE

WE MUST NOT ONLY GIVE
WHAT WE HAVE, WE MUST
ALSO GIVE WHAT WE ARE.

CARDINAL DÉSIRÉ-JOSEPH MERCIER

WHEN I WAS YOUNG,
I ADMIRED CLEVER PEOPLE.
NOW THAT I AM OLD, I ADMIRE
THOUGHTFUL PEOPLE.

ABRAHAM JOSHUA HESCHEL

IT MATTERS NOT HOW
LONG WE LIVE BUT HOW.

PHILIP JAMES BAILEY

WHAT WE'LL REMEMBER WHEN
WE'RE OLD ARE THE THINGS
WE DID FOR OTHERS.

WILL ROGERS

THANK YOU FOR *g*

A VERY IMPORTANT PART
OF THE JOY OF LIVING IS
THE JOY OF GIVING.

WILLIAM BUCK

NO PERSON WAS EVER
HONORED FOR WHAT HE RECEIVED.
HONOR HAS BEEN THE REWARD
FOR WHAT HE GAVE.

CALVIN COOLIDGE

FOR THIS I BLESS YOU MOST:
YOU GIVE MUCH AND KNOW NOT
THAT YOU GIVE AT ALL.

KHALIL GIBRAN

TREASURE THE ONE WHO
THINKS OF YOU WHEN ALL OTHERS
ARE THINKING OF THEMSELVES.

JAMES GUNN

THE WORLD KNOWS NOTHING
OF ITS GREATEST PEOPLE.

SIR HENRY TAYLOR

IT IS WHEN WE FORGET
OURSELVES THAT WE DO THINGS
THAT ARE MOST LIKELY
TO BE REMEMBERED.

UNKNOWN

BE A GO-GIVER AS
WELL AS A GO-GETTER.

UNKNOWN

LOCK YOUR HOUSE, GO ACROSS
THE RAILROAD TRACKS, FIND
SOMEONE IN NEED, AND DO
SOMETHING FOR HIM.

DR. KARL A. MENNINGER

JUST CONCENTRATE ON HELPING
ONE PERSON, GIVING HOPE TO
ONE PERSON, AND THAT PERSON IN
TURN MAY GIVE HOPE TO SOMEBODY
ELSE AND IT WILL SPREAD OUT.

AARON ABRAHAMSEN

CHARITY SEES THE NEED,
NOT THE CAUSE.

GERMAN PROVERB

VOLUNTEERS ARE THE ONLY
HUMAN BEINGS ON THE FACE OF THE
EARTH WHO REFLECT THIS NATION'S
COMPASSION, UNSELFISH CARING,
PATIENCE, AND JUST PLAIN LOVE
FOR ONE ANOTHER.

ERMA BOMBECK

WE MAKE A LIVING BY WHAT
WE GET, BUT WE MAKE A LIFE
BY WHAT WE GIVE.

HENRY BUCHER

WHAT A WONDERFUL MIRACLE,
IF ONLY WE COULD LOOK THROUGH
EACH OTHER'S EYES FOR AN INSTANT.

HENRY DAVID THOREAU

86

EMPATHY IS TWO HEARTS
PULLING AT ONE LOAD.

DAN ZADRA

IF WE COULD HEAR ONE
ANOTHER'S PRAYERS, IT WOULD
RELIEVE GOD OF A GREAT BURDEN.

MICHAEL NOLAN

IT IS IN FORGETTING OURSELVES
THAT WE ARE FOUND.

ST. FRANCIS OF ASSISI

THE INFINITE GOODNESS HAS
SUCH WIDE ARMS THAT IT TAKES
WHATEVER TURNS TO IT.

DANTE ALIGHIERI

WHAT WE FRANKLY GIVE,
FOREVER IS OUR OWN.

GEORGE GRANVILLE

THINK OF OTHER PEOPLE.
SERVE OTHER PEOPLE
SINCERELY. NO CHEATING.

THE DALAI LAMA

88

THE SERVICE WE RENDER TO
OTHERS IS REALLY THE RENT WE
PAY FOR OUR ROOM ON THIS EARTH.
THE PURPOSE OF THIS WORLD IS NOT
"TO HAVE AND TO HOLD" BUT "TO
GIVE AND SERVE." THERE CAN BE
NO OTHER MEANING.

SIR WILFRED T. GRENFELL

THE HEART OF THE GIVER MAKES
THE GIFT DEAR AND PRECIOUS.

MARTIN LUTHER

WHAT THE HEART GIVES AWAY
IS NEVER GONE. IT IS KEPT IN
THE HEARTS OF OTHERS.

ROBIN ST. JOHN

THE WORK OF OUR HEART,
THE WORK OF TAKING TIME, TO
LISTEN, TO HELP, IS ALSO OUR
GIFT TO THE WHOLE WORLD.

JACK KORNFIELD

MY LIFE IS MY MESSAGE.

MAHATMA GANDHI

A HERO IS SOMEONE
WHO HAS GIVEN HIS OR HER
LIFE TO SOMETHING BIGGER
THAN ONESELF.

JOSEPH CAMPBELL

90

DO YOU KNOW WHAT REAL
POVERTY IS? IT IS NEVER
HAVING A BIG THOUGHT OR
A GENEROUS IMPULSE.

JEROME P. FLEISHMAN

JUST KEEP PUTTING YOUR
LOVE OUT THERE.

UNKNOWN

DO A DEED OF SIMPLE KINDNESS,
THOUGH ITS END YOU MAY NOT SEE,
IT MAY REACH, LIKE WIDENING
RIPPLES, DOWN A LONG ETERNITY.

JOSEPH NORRIS

91

THE EFFECT OF ONE GOOD-HEARTED
PERSON IS INCALCULABLE.

ÓSCAR ARIAS

THE TRUE MEANING OF LIFE
IS TO PLANT TREES UNDER
WHOSE SHADE YOU DO
NOT EXPECT TO SIT.

NELSON HENDERSON

92

THE TEST OF THANKFULNESS
IS NOT WHAT YOU HAVE TO BE
THANKFUL FOR, BUT WHETHER
ANYONE ELSE HAS REASON TO BE
THANKFUL THAT YOU ARE HERE.

UNKNOWN

WE MUST CARE ABOUT THE
WORLD OF OUR CHILDREN AND
GRANDCHILDREN, A WORLD
WE MAY NEVER SEE.

BERTRAND RUSSELL

93

BEFORE MY DAUGHTER WAS BORN,
I WAS TEMPTED BY THE OVERALL
CYNICISM OF OUR AGE. BUT WHEN
YOU KNOW THAT YOUR CHILDREN
AND YOUR CHILDREN'S CHILDREN WILL
BE HERE AFTER YOU, YOU SUDDENLY
REALIZE THAT YOU HAVE A VERY
REAL RESPONSIBILITY TO
FUTURE GENERATIONS.

MARIANNE MOORE

THERE ARE ONLY SO
MANY TOMORROWS.

MICHAEL LANDON

94

TIME, INDEED,
IS A SACRED GIFT,
AND EACH DAY IS
A LITTLE LIFE.

SIR JOHN LUBBOCK

THE MIRACLE IS THIS—
THE MORE WE GIVE,
THE MORE WE HAVE.

ANONYMOUS

DON'T GIVE UP WHEN YOU
STILL HAVE SOMETHING TO GIVE.

UNKNOWN

ALL OUR ACTS HAVE
SACRAMENTAL POSSIBILITIES.

FREYA STARK

LIFE AND LOVE ARE ALL
WE GET, SO LIFE AND LOVE
ARE ALL WE CAN GIVE.

DAN ZADRA

THANK YOU FOR

erstanding

LIFE IS THE FIRST GIFT,
LOVE IS THE SECOND, AND
UNDERSTANDING THE THIRD.

MARGE PIERCY

98

HAVING SOMEONE WHO
UNDERSTANDS IS A GREAT BLESSING
FOR OURSELVES. BEING SOMEONE
WHO UNDERSTANDS IS A GREAT
BLESSING TO OTHERS.

JANETTE OKE

WHAT PEOPLE NEED IS A
GOOD LISTENING TO.

MARY LOU CASEY

IT TAKES A GREAT MAN TO
MAKE A GOOD LISTENER.

99

SIR ARTHUR HELPS

THERE IS NO GREATER
LOAN THAN A SYMPATHETIC EAR.

FRANK TYGER

I WISH I HAD ME TO LISTEN
TO WHEN I WAS 14.

ALANIS MORISSETTE

100

ONCE I GOT A FORTUNE COOKIE
THAT SAID, "TO REMEMBER IS TO
UNDERSTAND." A GOOD JUDGE
REMEMBERS WHAT IT WAS LIKE TO BE
A LAWYER. A GOOD BOSS REMEMBERS
WHAT IT WAS LIKE TO BE AN EMPLOYEE.
A GOOD PARENT REMEMBERS WHAT
IT WAS LIKE TO BE A CHILD.

ANNA QUINDLEN

PEOPLE CHANGE AND FORGET
TO TELL EACH OTHER.

LILLIAN HELLMAN

WHAT IS ACTUAL IS ACTUAL
ONLY FOR ONE TIME. AND
ONLY FOR ONE PLACE.

T.S. ELIOT

LOOK AT EACH PERSON YOU
MEET AS A PERSON IN PROGRESS.
THEN LOOK IN THE MIRROR AND SEE
ANOTHER PERSON IN PROGRESS.

CARL ROGERS

THEN I SAW YOU THROUGH
MYSELF AND FOUND WE
WERE IDENTICAL.

FAKHR AD-DIN

102

FRIENDSHIP BLOSSOMS WHEN
TWO PEOPLE SAY TO EACH OTHER,
IN EFFECT: "WHAT? YOU TOO?
I THOUGHT I WAS THE ONLY ONE!"

C.S. LEWIS

TO KNOW SOMEONE HERE OR
THERE WITH WHOM YOU CAN
FEEL THERE IS UNDERSTANDING IN
SPITE OF DISTANCES OR THOUGHTS
EXPRESSED—THAT CAN MAKE
LIFE A GARDEN.

JOHANN VON GOETHE

103

EVENTUALLY, IT'S THE SILENCES
WHICH MAKE THE REAL CONVERSATIONS
BETWEEN FRIENDS. NOT THE SAYING,
BUT THE NEVER NEEDING TO SAY.

MARGARET LEE RUNBECK

CRISES DO NOT MAKE FRIENDS—
THEY REVEAL THEM.

DON WARD

TROUBLE IS A PART OF LIFE,
AND IF YOU DON'T SHARE IT,
YOU DON'T GIVE THE PERSON
WHO LOVES YOU A CHANCE
TO LOVE YOU ENOUGH.

DINAH SHORE

THE LOVE OF OUR NEIGHBOR IN
ALL ITS FULLNESS SIMPLY MEANS
BEING ABLE TO SAY TO HIM, "WHAT
ARE YOU GOING THROUGH?"

SIMONE WEIL

EVERYONE HEARS WHAT YOU SAY.
FRIENDS LISTEN TO WHAT YOU SAY.
BEST FRIENDS LISTEN TO
WHAT YOU DON'T SAY.

UNKNOWN

THE HARDEST OF ALL IS TO
SHOW THEM WE LOVE THEM
NOT WHEN WE FEEL LIKE IT,
BUT WHEN THEY DO.

NAN FAIRBROTHER

MAYBE WE'RE FRIENDS NOT
BECAUSE OF ALL WE'VE SHARED
OR ALL WE KNOW ABOUT EACH
OTHER. MAYBE WHAT MAKES US
FRIENDS IS THAT DESPITE ALL
THAT, WE ARE STILL FRIENDS.

GLEN HERRINGTON-HALL

SOME OF THE MOST
SUCCESSFUL LEADERS ARE
ALSO THE BEST LISTENERS.

MARY KAY ASH

106

EMPATHY IS THE MASTER SKILL.

DAN ZADRA

IT'S EASIER FOR PEOPLE
TO SEE IT YOUR WAY IF YOU
FIRST SEE IT THEIR WAY.

JACK KAINE

NO ONE WANTS ADVICE,
WE WANT COLLABORATION.

RIAN JONES

LET PEOPLE ACCOMPLISH
YOUR OBJECTIVES THEIR WAY.

UNKNOWN

107

PEOPLE TEND TO RESIST THAT
WHICH IS FORCED UPON THEM.
PEOPLE TEND TO SUPPORT THAT
WHICH THEY HELP TO CREATE.

VINCE PFAFF

NOBODY IS PREFECT.

JULIE INGRAM

THERE ARE CHAPTERS
IN EVERY LIFE WHICH ARE
SELDOM READ AND
CERTAINLY NOT ALOUD.

CAROL SHIELDS

IF YOU JUDGE PEOPLE,
YOU HAVE NO TIME
TO LOVE THEM.

MOTHER TERESA

PEOPLE NEED YOUR LOVE
THE MOST WHEN THEY APPEAR
TO DESERVE IT LEAST.

JOHN HARRIGAN

BE ASSURED THAT IF
YOU KNEW ALL, YOU
WOULD PARDON ALL.

THOMAS À KEMPIS

ONE OF THE SECRETS OF
A LONG AND FRUITFUL LIFE
IS TO FORGIVE EVERYBODY
EVERYTHING EVERY NIGHT
BEFORE YOU GO TO BED.

BERNARD M. BARUCH

WE ARE ALL SPECIAL CASES.

ALBERT CAMUS

THE MOTTO SHOULD NOT BE,
"FORGIVE ONE ANOTHER." RATHER,
"UNDERSTAND ONE ANOTHER."

EMMA GOLDMAN

IF YOU DON'T KNOW THE KIND
OF PERSON I AM AND I DON'T KNOW
THE KIND OF PERSON YOU ARE A
PATTERN THAT OTHERS MADE MAY
PREVAIL IN THE WORLD AND
FOLLOWING THE WRONG GOD HOME
WE MAY MISS OUR STAR.

WILLIAM STAFFORD

SO MUCH OF OUR JOURNEY
IS LEARNING ABOUT AND
REMOVING BARRIERS.

MELODY BEATTIE

WE ALL LIVE WITH THE
OBJECTIVE OF BEING HAPPY;
OUR LIVES ARE ALL DIFFERENT
AND YET THE SAME.

ANNE FRANK

WE MAY NOT ALWAYS SEE
EYE-TO-EYE, BUT WE CAN TRY
TO SEE HEART-TO-HEART.

SAM LEVENSON

THANK YOU FOR

trusting

WE GROW IN TIME TO TRUST
THE FUTURE FOR OUR ANSWERS.

RUTH BENEDICT

FAITH AND DOUBT ARE NEEDED—
NOT AS ANTAGONISTS, BUT WORKING
SIDE BY SIDE—TO TAKE US AROUND
THE UNKNOWN CURVE.

LILLIAN SMITH

STILL ROUND THE CORNER
THERE MAY WAIT, A NEW ROAD
FOR YOU OR A SECRET GATE.

J.R.R. TOLKIEN

THERE CAN BE NO PROGRESS
UNLESS PEOPLE HAVE FAITH
IN TOMORROW.

JOHN F. KENNEDY

EVERY EXPERIENCE PREPARES
YOU FOR THE NEXT ONE.
YOU JUST DON'T EVER KNOW
WHAT THE NEXT ONE
IS GOING TO BE.

HOWARD SCHULTZ

SOMETIMES YOU KNOW
THE STORY. SOMETIMES YOU
MAKE IT UP AS YOU GO ALONG
AND HAVE NO IDEA HOW IT
WILL COME OUT.

ERNEST HEMINGWAY

THERE'S NO PLACE LIKE HOPE.

KOBI YAMADA

116

FAITH IN SMALL THINGS
HAS REPERCUSSIONS THAT RIPPLE
ALL THE WAY OUT. IN A HUGE,
DARK ROOM A LITTLE MATCH
CAN LIGHT UP THE PLACE.

JONI EARECKSON TADA

WE BUILD ON HOPE,
NOT ON FEAR.

EDMUND DAY

WE CANNOT BECOME
WHAT WE NEED TO BE BY
REMAINING WHAT WE ARE.

MAX DE PREE

THE WILLINGNESS TO CREATE
A NEW VISION IS A STATEMENT OF
YOUR BELIEF IN YOUR POTENTIAL.

DAVID McNALLY

YOU ARE THE ONE WHO CAN
STRETCH YOUR OWN HORIZON.

EDGAR F. MAGNIN

TRUST COMES FROM KEEPING
A SERIES OF COMMITMENTS.

DEANNA BERG

WE HAVE TO BE ABLE TO
COUNT ON EACH OTHER DOING
WHAT WE HAVE AGREED TO DO.

PHIL CROSBY

TRUST EACH OTHER AGAIN
AND AGAIN—AND YOU WILL
BUILD A GREAT TEAM.

DAVID ARMISTEAD

YOU CAN WORK MIRACLES
BY HAVING FAITH IN OTHERS.
TO INSPIRE THE BEST IN PEOPLE,
CHOOSE TO THINK AND BELIEVE
THE BEST ABOUT THEM.

BOB MOAWAD

119

TRUST IS THE CONVICTION
THAT THE LEADER MEANS WHAT
HE OR SHE SAYS. IT IS A BELIEF
IN TWO OLD-FASHIONED QUALITIES
CALLED CONSISTENCY AND
INTEGRITY. TRUST OPENS THE
DOOR TO CHANGE.

PETER DRUCKER

WE ALWAYS
UNDERESTIMATE THE FUTURE.

CHARLES F. KETTERING

DOWN DEEP IN EVERY HUMAN
SOUL IS A HIDDEN LONGING,
IMPULSE, AND AMBITION TO DO
SOMETHING FINE AND ENDURING.

GRENVILLE KLEISER

THE WILL TO DO,
THE SOUL TO DARE.

SIR WALTER SCOTT

MAN CAN LEARN NOTHING
EXCEPT BY GOING FROM THE
KNOWN TO THE UNKNOWN.

CLAUDE BERNARD

WHEN WE WALK TO THE EDGE
OF ALL THE LIGHT WE HAVE, AND
MUST TAKE A STEP INTO THE DARKNESS
OF THE UNKNOWN, WE MUST BELIEVE
THAT ONE OF TWO THINGS WILL HAPPEN.
EITHER THERE WILL BE SOMETHING
SOLID FOR US TO STAND ON OR WE
WILL BE TAUGHT HOW TO FLY.

PATRICK OVERTON

WE REALLY BECOME HUMAN
AT THE POINT OF REACHING OUT
AND RISKING AND TRUSTING
TO BRING PEOPLE IN.

KOBI YAMADA

IF I CAN COUNT ON YOU,
AND YOU CAN COUNT ON ME,
JUST THINK WHAT A WONDERFUL
WORLD THIS WILL BE!

CHILDHOOD RHYME

PEOPLE WHO DEAL WITH LIFE
GENEROUSLY AND LARGE-HEARTEDLY
GO ON MULTIPLYING
RELATIONSHIPS TO THE END.

A.C. BENSON

THE WAY IS LONG—LET US
GO TOGETHER. THE WAY IS
DIFFICULT—LET US HELP EACH
OTHER. THE WAY IS JOYFUL—
LET US SHARE IT.

JOYCE HUNTER

WE HAVE A LIMITED
NUMBER OF HEARTBEATS
AND WE'RE IN CHARGE OF
HOW WE USE THEM.

PETER ALSOP

SO HOLD ON TO THE
ONES WHO REALLY CARE.
IN THE END THEY'LL BE
THE ONLY ONES STILL THERE.

HANSON

HERALD THE DAY WHEN WE
CAN ALWAYS APPRECIATE
ONE ANOTHER.

DES'REE

EVERY LITTLE BLESSING
IS FAR TOO PRECIOUS TO EVER
FORGET TO SAY "THANK YOU!"

LAURA REGIS

GRATITUDE UNLOCKS
THE FULLNESS OF LIFE.
IT TURNS WHAT WE HAVE
INTO ENOUGH, AND MORE.

MELODY BEATTIE

GRATITUDE IS THE
MEMORY OF THE HEART.

JEAN-BAPTISTE MASSIEU

MAY HAPPINESS TOUCH
YOUR LIFE TODAY AS WARMLY
AS YOU HAVE TOUCHED THE
LIVES OF OTHERS.

REBECCA FORSYTHE

125

YOUR HEART HAS BROUGHT
GREAT JOY TO MANY.
THOSE HEARTS CAN
NEVER FORGET YOU.

FLAVIA WEEDEN

THANK YOU FOR

OTHER "GIFT OF INSPIRATION" BOOKS AVAILABLE:

Be Happy
Remember to live, love,
laugh and learn

Be the Difference

Because of You
Celebrating the Difference You Make

Brilliance
Uncommon voices from
uncommon women

Commitment to Excellence
Celebrating the Very Best

Diversity
Celebrating the Differences

Everyone Leads
It takes each of us to make
a difference for all of us

Expect Success
Our Commitment to Our Customer

Forever Remembered
A Gift for the Grieving Heart

I Believe in You
To your heart, your dream,
and the difference you make

Little Miracles
Cherished messages of hope,
joy, love, kindness and courage

Never Quit
Inspiring Insights on Courage
& Commitment

Reach for the Stars
Give up the good to go for the great

Team Works
Working Together Works

To Your Success
Thoughts to Give Wings to
Your Work and Your Dreams

Together We Can
Celebrating the power of a
team and a dream

Welcome Home
Celebrating the Best Place on Earth

What's Next
Creating the Future Now

Whatever It Takes
A Journey into the Heart
of Human Achievement

You've Got a Friend
Thoughts to Celebrate the
Joy of Friendship